REGIONS OF THE
UNITED STATES

REM 1142

WRITTEN BY: **Betty J. Peterson**

A TEACHING RESOURCE FROM

REMEDIA PUBLICATIONS

www.rempub.com

REMEDIA PUBLICATIONS, INC.
SCOTTSDALE, AZ

RESEARCH-BASED ACTIVITIES
Supports State & National Standards

This product utilizes innovative strategies and proven methods to improve student learning. The product is based upon reliable research and effective practices that have been replicated in classrooms across the United States. Information regarding the research basis is provided on our website at www.rempub.com/research

Introduction

Activities in this book have been designed to help students learn the states and capitals as well as some related facts. Maps are simple and not cluttered with unrelated lines and features. Material is repeated in different ways, providing lots of practice and many opportunities for learning.

States have been grouped into eight regions. Five pages have been devoted to each group:

1. A map of the region to be filled in with colored pencils.

2. A map of the region for students to match locations to names.

3. A crossword puzzle.

4. Information about states in the region followed by questions.

5. Vertical puzzle or word search puzzle.

A map of the United States, pre/post test, and state data sheet have also been included.

Regions of the U.S. — Answer Key

PAGE 1: Map locations/states and their capitals: Augusta, Maine; Montpelier, Vermont; Concord, New Hampshire; Boston, Massachusetts; Hartford, Connecticut; Providence, Rhode Island

PAGE 2: A) Maine B) New Hampshire C) Vermont D) Massachusetts E) Connecticut F) Rhode Island 1) Augusta 2) Concord 3) Montpelier 4) Boston 5) Hartford 6) Providence

PAGE 3: ACROSS: 3) Massachusetts 6) Rhode Island 7) Maine 8) Boston 12) Vermont 13) Hartford DOWN: 1) New Hampshire 2) Connecticut 4) Augusta 5) Concord 9) Atlantic 10) Providence 11) Montpelier

PAGE 4: 1) Massachusetts 2) Rhode Island 3) Maine 4) Massachusetts 5) Connecticut 6) Vermont 7) Rhode Island 8) New Hampshire 9) Maine 10) Vermont

PAGE 5: 1) Pilgrims 2) Maine 3) Plymouth Rock 4) Colonial 5) Vermont 6) Cape Cod 7) Providence 8) Connecticut 9) Hartford 10) granite Vertical box: Paul Revere

PAGE 6: Map locations: Lake Ontario borders New York; Lake Erie borders New York and Pennsylvania on this map; Hudson River runs north and south through New York; Atlantic Ocean is east (to the right) of Mid-Atlantic states; Washington, D.C. is on border of Maryland, indicated by star; States and their capitals: Albany, New York; Harrisburg, Pennsylvania; Trenton, New Jersey; Dover, Delaware; Annapolis, Maryland

PAGE 7: A) New York B) Pennsylvania C) New Jersey D) Delaware E) Maryland 1) Albany 2) Harrisburg 3) Trenton 4) Dover 5) Annapolis

PAGE 8: ACROSS: 3) Pennsylvania 6) New Jersey 8) Annapolis 9) Delaware 11) Dover 12) New York DOWN: 1) Albany 2) Washington, D.C. 4) Maryland 5) Atlantic 7) Harrisburg 10) Trenton

PAGE 9: 1) New York 2) New Jersey 3) Pennsylvania 4) Maryland 5) New York 6) Delaware 7) Delaware 8) Delaware 9) Maryland 10) Washington, D.C. 11) Pennsylvania 12) Washington, D.C.

PAGE 10: 1) Maryland 2) Harrisburg 3) Delaware 4) Washington, D.C. 5) Albany 6) Maryland 7) Annapolis 8) First 9) Atlantic 10) Lake Erie 11) capital 12) Hershey Vertical Box: Niagara Falls

PAGE 11: Map locations: Gulf of Mexico is located west (to the left) of Florida; Atlantic Ocean runs along the east coast (to the right) of the South Atlantic states; Appalachian Mountains run through West Virginia, Virginia and North Carolina; States and their capitals: Charleston, West Virginia; Richmond, Virginia; Raleigh, North Carolina; Columbia, South Carolina; Atlanta, Georgia; Tallahassee, Florida

PAGE 12: A) West Virginia B) Virginia C) North Carolina D) South Carolina E) Georgia F) Florida 1) Charleston 2) Richmond 3) Raleigh 4) Columbia 5) Atlanta 6) Tallahassee

PAGE 13: ACROSS: 1) Tallahassee 5) Georgia 8) Columbia 11) South Carolina 13) West Virginia DOWN: 2) Appalachian 3) Florida 4) Virginia 6) Richmond 7) North Carolina 9) Raleigh 10) Charleston 12) Atlanta

PAGE 14: 1) Florida 2) West Virginia 3) Virginia 4) North Carolina 5) North Carolina 6) South Carolina 7) Florida 8) West Virginia 9) Florida 10) Georgia 11) Virginia 12) South Carolina

PAGE 15: 1) Gulf of Mexico 2) Raleigh 3) Georgia 4) West Virginia 5) Mount Vernon 6) Cape Canaveral 7) Kitty Hawk 8) Florida 9) Richmond 10) Atlanta 11) South Carolina 12) Newport News

PAGE 16: Map locations: Lake Michigan runs between Wisconsin and Michigan; Lake Huron borders Michigan; Lake Superior borders Wisconsin and Michigan's upper peninsula; Lake Erie borders Ohio; Ohio River borders Ohio, Indiana and the tip of Illinois; Mississippi River borders Wisconsin and Illinois States and their capitals: Madison, Wisconsin; Springfield, Illinois; Indianapolis, Indiana; Lansing, Michigan; Columbus, Ohio

PAGE 17: A) Wisconsin B) Michigan C) Illinois D) Indiana E) Ohio 1) Madison 2) Lansing 3) Springfield 4) Indianapolis 5) Columbus

PAGE 18: ACROSS: 1) Indianapolis 4) Mississippi 5) Indiana 9) Superior 11) Columbus 12) Michigan 13) Michigan DOWN: 1) Illinois 2) Springfield 3) Madison 6) Erie 7) Wisconsin 8) Lansing 10) Ohio

PAGE 19: 1) Indiana 2) Wisconsin 3) Sears Tower, Illinois 4) Ohio 5) Detroit 6) Indiana 7) O'Hare, Chicago 8) Mackinac Bridge 9) Illinois 10) astronaut 11) Hoosiers 12) Wisconsin

PAGE 20: 1) Wisconsin 2) Madison 3) Indiana 4) Springfield 5) Armstrong 6) Mackinac 7) Gary 8) peninsulas 9) Ohio 10) Lansing 11) Chicago 12) Sears Tower Vertical box: Indianapolis

PAGE 21: Map locations: Gulf of Mexico borders eastern Texas and southern Louisiana; Appalachian Mountains run through Tennessee; Ozark Mountains run through northern Arkansas; Mississippi River runs along border of Arkansas and through Louisiana to the Gulf; Rio Grande River runs along southwestern border of Texas into Gulf States and their capitals: Frankfort, Kentucky; Nashville, Tennessee; Montgomery, Alabama; Jackson, Mississippi; Little Rock, Arkansas; Baton Rouge, Louisiana; Oklahoma City, Oklahoma; Austin, Texas

PAGE 22: A) Kentucky B) Tennessee C) Alabama D) Mississippi E) Arkansas F) Louisiana G) Oklahoma H) Texas   1) Frankfort 2) Nashville 3) Montgomery 4) Jackson 5) Little Rock 6) Baton Rouge 7) Oklahoma City 8) Austin

PAGE 23: ACROSS: 1) Tennessee 3) Oklahoma 5) Jackson 9) Austin 10) Little Rock 11) Mississippi 12) Rio Grande 13) Montgomery   DOWN: 1) Texas 2) Baton Rouge 4) Kentucky 6) Nashville 7) Alabama 8) Louisiana 14) Ozark

PAGE 24: 1) Fort Knox, Kentucky 2) Nashville, Tennessee 3) Arkansas 4) Lookout Mountain, Tennessee 5) New Orleans, Louisiana 6) Texas 7) Birmingham, Alabama 8) Mississippi 9) Tulsa, Oklahoma

PAGE 25: 1) Arkansas 2) Nashville 3) Mississippi 4) Jackson 5) Ozark 6) Baton Rouge 7) Louisiana 8) Montgomery 9) Kentucky 10) Little Rock 11) Texas 12) Oklahoma 13) Alabama 14) Mexico 15) Austin 16) Rio Grande 17) Appalachian

PAGE 26: Map locations: Mississippi River starts in Minnesota and runs along the borders of Minnesota, Iowa and Missouri; Missouri River starts in South Dakota and runs along border of Nebraska into Missouri; Lake Superior borders Minnesota on the northeast; the Black Hills run along the western border of South Dakota; Ozark Mountains are in southern Missouri; States and their capitals: Bismarck, North Dakota; Pierre, South Dakota; Lincoln, Nebraska; Topeka, Kansas; Jefferson City, Missouri; Des Moines, Iowa; St. Paul, Minnesota

PAGE 27: A) Minnesota B) Iowa C) Missouri D) North Dakota E) South Dakota F) Nebraska G) Kansas   1) St. Paul 2) Des Moines 3) Jefferson City 4) Bismarck 5) Pierre 6) Lincoln 7) Topeka

PAGE 28: ACROSS: 4) North Dakota 5) Missouri 8) St. Paul 11) Nebraska 12) Minnesota 13) Bismarck 14) Jefferson City   DOWN: 1) South Dakota 2) Kansas 3) Pierre 6) Iowa 7) Des Moines 9) Topeka 10) Lincoln

PAGE 29: 1) South Dakota 2) Minnesota 3) Kansas 4) Minnesota 5) South Dakota 6) Kansas 7) North Dakota 8) Iowa 9) Nebraska 10) Missouri

PAGE 30: 1) Missouri 2) Mayo Clinic 3) South Dakota 4) Kansas 5) North Dakota 6) Nebraska 7) Gold Rush 8) Des Moines 9) Eisenhower 10) monument 11) Omaha 12) Superior 13) Breadbasket   Vertical box: Mount Rushmore

PAGE 31: Map locations: Rocky Mountains extend from Montana to New Mexico; Great Salt Lake is located in the northwest corner of Utah; Colorado River starts in Colorado and runs along border of Arizona; States and their capitals: Helena, Montana; Boise, Idaho; Cheyenne, Wyoming; Denver, Colorado; Salt Lake City, Utah; Carson City, Nevada; Phoenix, Arizona; Santa Fe, New Mexico

PAGE 32: A) Montana B) Idaho C) Wyoming D) Nevada E) Utah F) Colorado G) Arizona H) New Mexico   1) Helena 2) Boise 3) Cheyenne 4) Carson City 5) Salt Lake City 6) Denver 7) Phoenix 8) Santa Fe

PAGE 33: ACROSS: 3) Colorado River 6) Rocky 7) Nevada 9) Utah 12) Wyoming 14) Phoenix 15) Salt Lake City 17) Carson City   DOWN: 1) Montana 2) Arizona 3) Colorado 4) Idaho 5) Denver 8) New Mexico 10) Helena 11) Boise 13) Santa Fe 16) Cheyenne

PAGE 34: 1) Wyoming 2) Arizona 3) Denver, Colorado 4) Utah 5) Montana 6) Nevada 7) New Mexico 8) Utah 9) Arizona 10) Idaho

PAGE 35: 1) Montana 2) Nevada 3) Idaho 4) New Mexico 5) Rocky Mountains 6) Great Salt Lake 7) Phoenix 8) Utah 9) Helena 10) Carson City 11) Denver 12) Santa Fe 13) Cheyenne 14) Arizona 15) Wyoming 16) Boise 17) Colorado

PAGE 36: Map locations: Mt. McKinley is located in Alaska; Columbia River runs through the state of Washington and west along the Oregon/Washington border; Pacific Ocean borders the Pacific States on the west (left); Yukon River is located in Alaska; States and their capitals: Juneau, Alaska; Olympia, Washington; Salem, Oregon; Sacramento, California; Honolulu, Hawaiian Islands

PAGE 37: A) Alaska B) Washington C) Oregon D) California E) Hawaiian Islands 1) Juneau 2) Olympia 3) Salem 4) Sacramento 5) Honolulu

PAGE 38: ACROSS: 1) California 4) Honolulu 8) Sacramento 9) Alaska 10) Juneau 11) Yukon 12) Oregon   DOWN: 1) Columbia 2) Olympia 3) Washington 4) Hawaii 5) Salem 6) McKinley 7) Pacific

PAGE 39: 1) California 2) Oregon 3) Alaska 4) Hawaii 5) Washington 6) California 7) Hawaii 8) Alaska 9) Washington 10) Oregon 11) volcanoes 12) Russia

PAGE 40: 1) Washington 2) Olympia 3) Pacific 4) Yukon River 5) Juneau 6) McKinley 7) Disneyland 8) Oregon 9) Crater Lake 10) volcanoes   Vertical box: Sacramento

Write as many of the states and their capitals as you can.

1. _____ / _____
2. _____ / _____
3. _____ / _____
4. _____ / _____
5. _____ / _____
6. _____ / _____
7. _____ / _____
8. _____ / _____
9. _____ / _____
10. _____ / _____
11. _____ / _____
12. _____ / _____
13. _____ / _____
14. _____ / _____
15. _____ / _____
16. _____ / _____
17. _____ / _____
18. _____ / _____
19. _____ / _____
20. _____ / _____
21. _____ / _____
22. _____ / _____
23. _____ / _____
24. _____ / _____
25. _____ / _____
26. _____ / _____
27. _____ / _____

Name _____

28. _____ / _____

29. _____ / _____

30. _____ / _____

31. _____ / _____

32. _____ / _____

33. _____ / _____

34. _____ / _____

35. _____ / _____

36. _____ / _____

37. _____ / _____

38. _____ / _____

39. _____ / _____

40. _____ / _____

41. _____ / _____

42. _____ / _____

43. _____ / _____

44. _____ / _____

45. _____ / _____

46. _____ / _____

47. _____ / _____

48. _____ / _____

49. _____ / _____

50. _____ / _____

How many states and capitals did you know before you studied this unit?

Pre-Test: States _____ Capitals _____

How many states and capitals did you know after you studied this unit?

Post-Test: States _____ Capitals _____

Regions of the United States

New England States

1. **Write the name of each state, city, body of water, or mountain range in its correct location on the map below. Use colored pencils.**

RED	GREEN	BLACK
Maine	Hartford	Atlantic Ocean
New Hampshire	Boston	
Vermont	Concord	
Connecticut	Montpelier	
Rhode Island	Augusta	
Massachusetts	Providence	

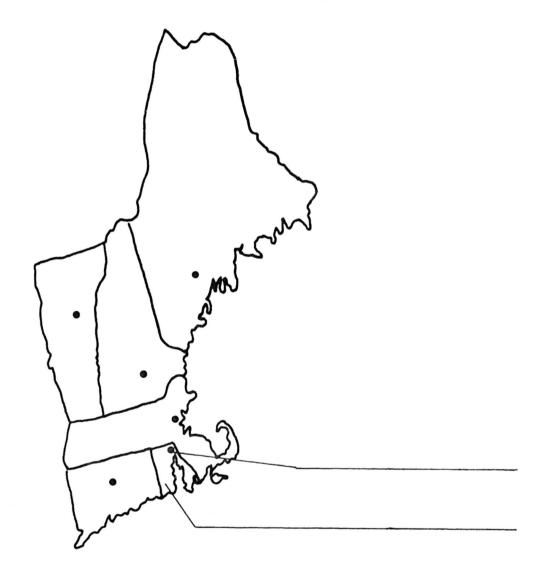

2. **With colored pencils, shade in each state:** Maine (purple); New Hampshire (green); Connecticut (blue); Vermont (yellow); Massachusetts (orange); Rhode Island (brown).

Regions of the United States

Name _____

New England States

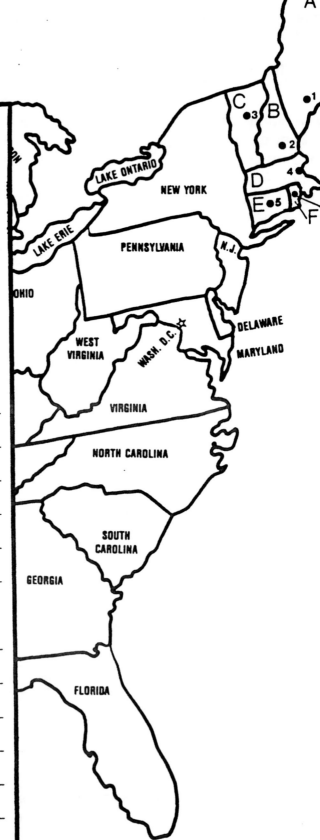

Match each location to its correct letter or numeral.

LOCATIONS

Providence	Augusta
Montpelier	Vermont
Maine	Concord
New Hampshire	Massachusetts
Connecticut	Rhode Island
Hartford	Boston

STATES

A. _____

B. _____

C. _____

D. _____

E. _____

F. _____

CAPITALS

1. _____

2. _____

3. _____

4. _____

5. _____

6. _____

2

Name _____

New England States

ACROSS CLUES:
3. state north of Connecticut
6. smallest state in the U.S.
7. most northern state
8. capital of Massachusetts
12. state west of New Hampshire
13. capital of Connecticut

DOWN CLUES:
1. state east of Vermont
2. state west of Rhode Island
4. capital of Maine
5. capital of New Hampshire
9. ocean to the east of Massachusetts
10. capital of Rhode Island
11. capital of Vermont

3

New England States

Maine is a leading potato-producing state. These potatoes are grown in Aroostook County in northern Maine. Maine leads the United States in the number of lobsters trapped each year. This state is also famous for its beautiful, rocky coast.

Massachusetts gets its name from the Massachusett Indian tribe. The Pilgrims came from England on the Mayflower in 1620 and landed at Plymouth Rock. Many important events of the American Revolution took place in Massachusetts. These included the Boston Tea Party and the famous ride of Paul Revere. The Cape Cod area is famous for tourism and cranberries.

Rhode Island is our smallest state. Rhode Island Red chickens are world-famous and were developed in 1854. Roger Williams is known as "The Father of Rhode Island." He and his followers were seeking religious freedom.

New Hampshire is famous for its natural beauty and year-round outdoor activities. In the winter, people enjoy skiing, winter carnivals, and dog sled races. In the fall, people love to see the countryside ablaze with red, yellow, and orange leaves.

Connecticut is an important manufacturing state. Aircraft engines, propellers, helicopters, and submarines are some products manufactured here. Over half the people work in manufacturing or related industries. Nearly every town has a colonial building which is interesting to visit.

Vermont produces more maple syrup than any other state. In late winter and early spring, the trees are tapped for sap. Three-fourths of the land is covered with forests. Vermont has the largest granite quarries in the world. Granite is used in monuments and public buildings. The beautiful Green Mountains make Vermont a popular tourist state.

Name That State . . .

1. place where Pilgrims landed:

   _____

2. famous chickens raised here:

   _____

3. leading producer of potatoes:

   _____

4. good place to pick cranberries:

   _____

5. important manufacturing state:

   _____

6. home of largest granite quarries:

   _____

7. our smallest state:

   _____

8. has beautiful autumn scenery:

   _____

9. famous lobster-producing state:

   _____

10. eat pancakes with maple syrup here:

   _____

Name _____

New England States

Complete this puzzle with answers to the questions below.

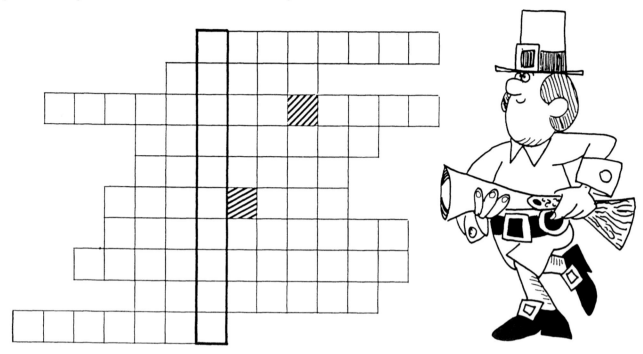

1. We came from England on the Mayflower. Who are we?
2. I am the most northern state. What state am I?
3. I am the place where the Pilgrims first landed. What place am I?
4. I am a type of building found in almost every town in Connecticut. What type of building am I?
5. I am a state west of New Hampshire. What state am I?
6. I am a famous tourist area in Massachusetts. What is my name?
7. I am the capital of Rhode Island. What is my name?
8. I am the state south of Massachusetts. What state am I?
9. I am the capital of Connecticut. What is my name?
10. I am a type of rock found in Vermont. I am used to build monuments and public buildings. What type of rock am I?

I am known for my famous horseback ride through Boston, Massachusetts. Who am I?
(letters in the vertical box on the puzzle spell the answer)

_____

5

Regions of the United States

Name _____

Mid-Atlantic States

1. **Write the name of each state, city, body of water, or mountain range in its correct location on the map below. Use colored pencils.**

RED	GREEN	BLACK
New York	Harrisburg	Atlantic Ocean
Pennsylvania	Trenton	Lake Ontario
Delaware	Annapolis	Lake Erie
New Jersey	Albany	Hudson River
Maryland	Dover	Washington, D.C.

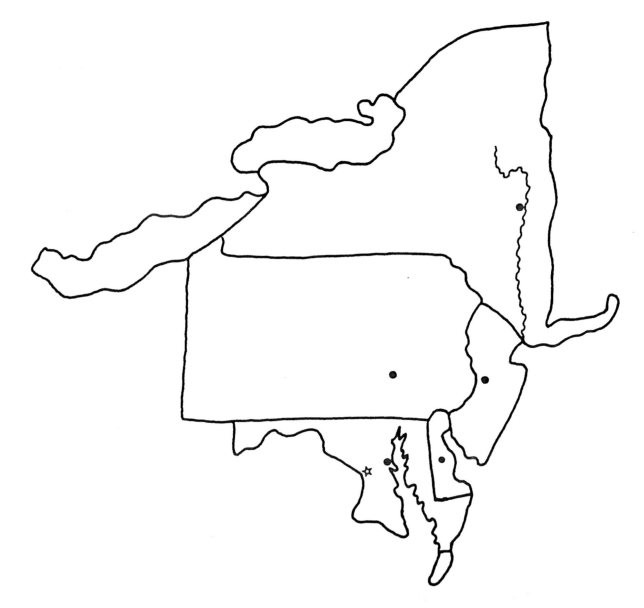

2. **With a colored pencil, shade in each state:** New York (purple); Pennsylvania (yellow); New Jersey (green); Delaware (blue); Maryland (orange).

6

Name _____

Mid-Atlantic States

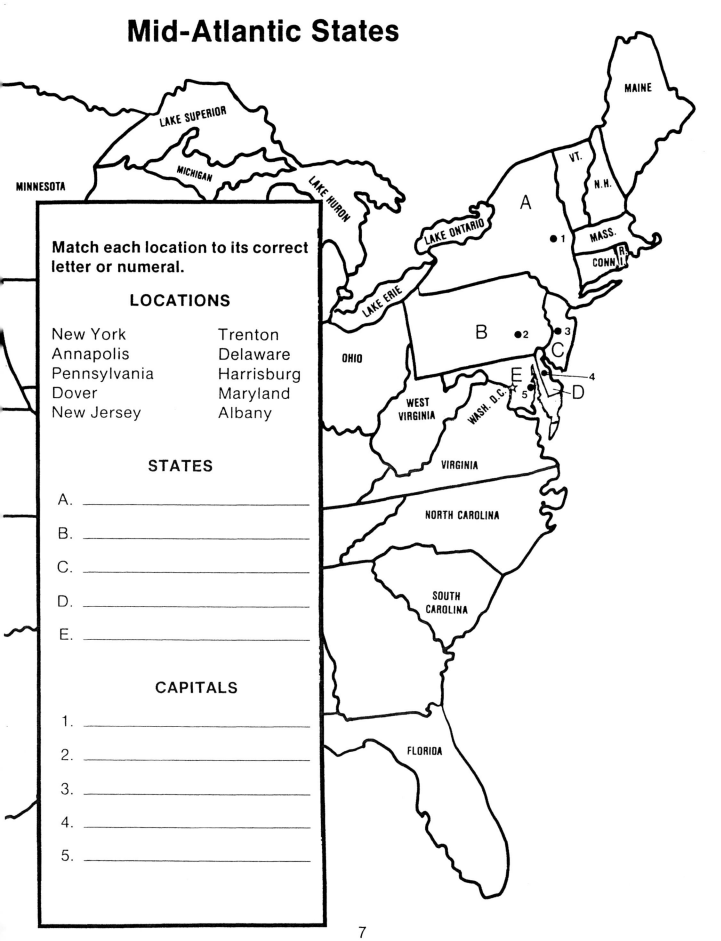

Match each location to its correct letter or numeral.

LOCATIONS

New York   Trenton
Annapolis   Delaware
Pennsylvania   Harrisburg
Dover   Maryland
New Jersey   Albany

STATES

A. _____

B. _____

C. _____

D. _____

E. _____

CAPITALS

1. _____

2. _____

3. _____

4. _____

5. _____

7

Regions of the United States

Mid-Atlantic States

ACROSS CLUES:

3. state south of New York
6. state east of Pennsylvania
8. capital of Maryland
9. state east of Maryland
11. capital of Delaware
12. state north of Pennsylvania

DOWN CLUES:

1. capital of New York
2. capital of the United States
4. state north of Virginia
5. ocean east of Delaware
7. capital of Pennsylvania
10. capital of New Jersey

8

Mid-Atlantic States

New York is a land of fertile river valleys and sparkling lakes. The state's most famous natural wonder is Niagara Falls, the "Honeymooners' Paradise." In the harbor of New York City is the Statue of Liberty. The capital of this state is Albany.

New Jersey has many beaches and popular summer resorts. The capital city is Trenton. New Jersey's many truck farms, orchards, and flower gardens give it the nickname, "The Garden State."

Delaware is the second smallest state. It has often been called "The First State" because it was the first state to approve the United States Constitution. Its capital is Dover. Delaware is a leading state in the raising of broilers (chickens).

Washington, D.C., is the capital of the United States. Every year millions of people go to Washington, D.C. They visit the Washington Monument, the Capitol, and the White House.

Maryland leads all states in the production of oysters. Chesapeake Bay is a place where people can enjoy boating, fishing, and swimming. Annapolis, the capital, is the home of the United States Naval Academy.

Pennsylvania was named after William Penn who began a colony for Quakers there in 1681. The world's largest chocolate factory is in Hershey. Pennsylvania is a leading state in the production of steel.

Where would you find . . .

1. the Statue of Liberty?

   _____

2. the Garden State?

   _____

3. the largest chocolate factory?

   _____

4. the U.S. Naval Academy?

   _____

5. Niagara Falls?

   _____

6. the second smallest state?

   _____

7. broilers (chickens)?

   _____

8. the city of Dover?

   _____

9. oysters?

   _____

10. the White House?

    _____

11. steel mills?

    _____

12. the nation's capital?

    _____

9

Mid-Atlantic States

Complete this puzzle with answers to the questions below.

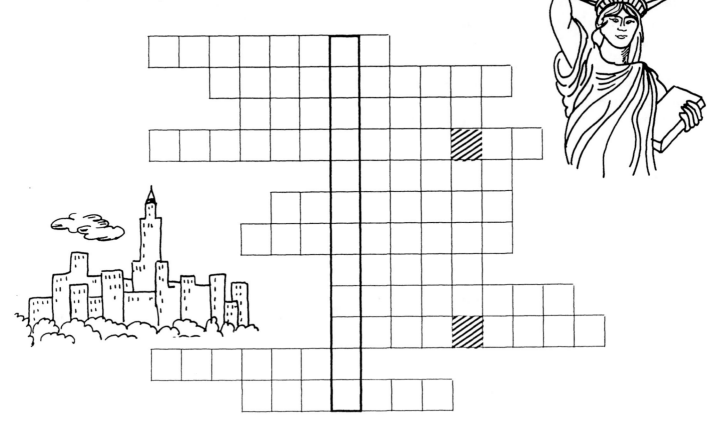

1. My capital is Annapolis. What state am I?
2. I am the capital of Pennsylvania. What is my name?
3. I am the state east of Maryland. What state am I?
4. I am the capital of the United States. What is my name?
5. I am the capital of New York. What is my name?
6. I am a state directly north of Virginia. What is my name?
7. I am the capital of Maryland. What is my name?
8. My name is Delaware. I am called "The _____ State."
9. I am an ocean east of Delaware. What ocean am I?
10. I am one of the Great Lakes. What is my name?
11. My name is Washington, D.C. I am called the nation's _____.
12. I am the home of the world's largest chocolate factory. What is my name?

What famous tourist attraction in New York is known as "Honeymooners' Paradise"?
(letters in the vertical box on the puzzle spell the answer)

_____

South Atlantic States

1. **Write the name of each state, city, body of water, or mountain range in its correct location on the map below. Use colored pencils.**

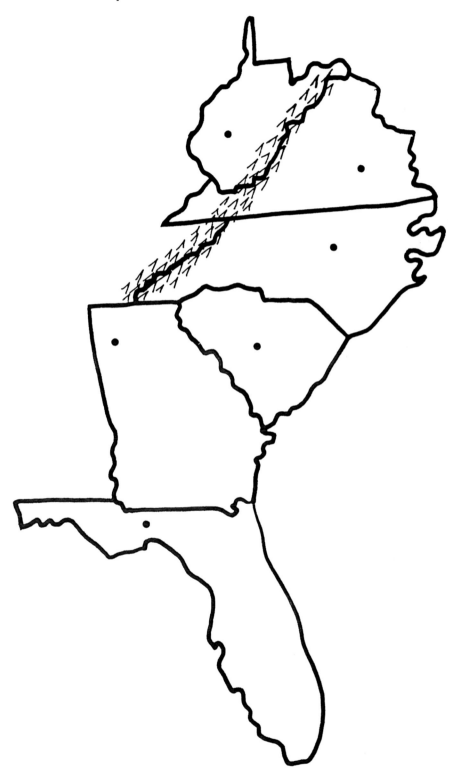

RED
West Virginia
Virginia
North Carolina
South Carolina
Florida
Georgia

GREEN
Atlanta
Tallahassee
Columbia
Richmond
Raleigh
Charleston

BLACK
Gulf of Mexico
Appalachian Mountains
Atlantic Ocean

2. **With colored pencils, shade in each state:** Virginia (green); South Carolina (brown); Florida (yellow); North Carolina (blue); West Virginia (pink); Georgia (purple).

11

Regions of the United States

South Atlantic States

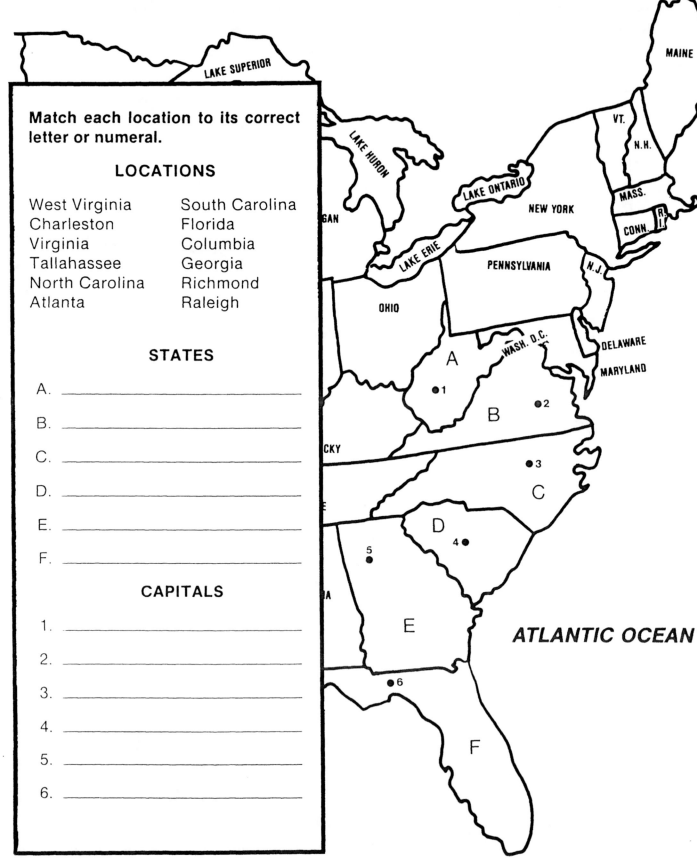

Match each location to its correct letter or numeral.

LOCATIONS

West Virginia	South Carolina
Charleston	Florida
Virginia	Columbia
Tallahassee	Georgia
North Carolina	Richmond
Atlanta	Raleigh

STATES

A. _____

B. _____

C. _____

D. _____

E. _____

F. _____

CAPITALS

1. _____

2. _____

3. _____

4. _____

5. _____

6. _____

ATLANTIC OCEAN

12

South Atlantic States

ACROSS CLUES:

1. capital of Florida
5. state north of Florida
8. capital of South Carolina
11. state northeast of Georgia
13. state northwest of Virginia

DOWN CLUES:

2. mountains in eastern U.S.
3. state south of Georgia
4. state north of North Carolina
6. capital of Virginia
7. state south of Virginia
9. capital of North Carolina
10. capital of West Virginia
12. capital of Georgia

13

South Atlantic States

Florida is a leading tourist state. People visit this state to see the Space Center at Cape Canaveral and Epcot Center and Disney World near Orlando. Other popular places include Everglades National Park and St. Augustine, the oldest city in the United States. Lots of oranges and grapefruit are grown in Florida.

Virginia is a historic state. Here you can see Mount Vernon, the home of George Washington. Williamsburg is a city restored to look like the 1700's. One of the world's largest shipyards is at Newport News. The Blue Ridge Mountains are in Virginia.

West Virginia is often called "The Mountain State." The mountains are filled with tumbling rivers and rugged forests. There are many coal mines in West Virginia.

North Carolina is the leading tobacco state. Kitty Hawk is the site of the world's first airplane flight by the Wright Brothers. There are many famous battlefields in North Carolina.

Georgia is the leading peanut-producing state. The hometown of former President Jimmy Carter is Plains. Interesting sights in Georgia include towering pine trees, peach groves, magnolias, mossy trees, and marble and granite quarries.

South Carolina is the place to see many beautiful, old Southern plantations and lots of lovely beaches and gardens. Fort Sumter, site of the opening battle of the Civil War, is in South Carolina.

Where would you go to see . . .

1. Disney World?

   _____

2. coal mines?

   _____

3. Blue Ridge Mountains?

   _____

4. Kitty Hawk?

   _____

5. tobacco fields?

   _____

6. Southern plantations?

   _____

7. Cape Canaveral?

   _____

8. "The Mountain State"?

   _____

9. oldest city in the U.S.?

   _____

10. leading peanut state?

    _____

11. George Washington's home?

    _____

12. Fort Sumter?

    _____

South Atlantic States

```
N E S P A B G U L F O F M E X I C O L F
O W V I C A E G N I A T E R N E A B C L
D T K L M A O E G U O F L R A P P U Y O
W E S T V I R G I N I A S V E D E L M R
N G E R T A G S L O M A N I J K C E S I
T A B I C A I R U F K I T T Y H A W K D
V E D A L R A L E I G H R G A B N C F A
I R B M O I N P U Q V S X A T L A N T A
T A R Y W C C E I B G I H N H Z V D M F
K S O U T H C A R O L I N A P L E Q U T
A R E S Y M C V Z M O U N T V E R N O N
G I W I S O J E F T R X V P B T A H X O
T U N D H N E W P O R T N E W S L A N T
A K A S A D Y L A Q F U M L V S G E O R
```

Use these clues to find and circle the hidden words in the puzzle above.

1. I am a body of water south of Florida.
2. I am the capital of North Carolina.
3. I am the home state of Jimmy Carter.
4. I am a state where there is a lot of coal mining.
5. I am the home of George Washington.
6. I am the site of the Space Center.
7. I am the site of the world's first airplane flight.
8. I am the state in which Disney World is located.
9. I am the capital of Virginia.
10. I am the capital of Georgia.
11. I am the state in which Ft. Sumter is located.
12. I am the home of the world's largest shipyard.

15

Eastern North Central States

1. **Write the name of each state, city, body of water, or mountain range in its correct location on the map below. Use colored pencils.**

RED	GREEN	BLACK
Wisconsin	Lansing	Lake Superior
Michigan	Springfield	Lake Michigan
Ohio	Madison	Lake Huron
Indiana	Columbus	Lake Erie
Illinois	Indianapolis	Ohio River
		Mississippi River

2. **With colored pencils, shade in each state:** Ohio (yellow); Illinois (blue); Indiana (brown); Wisconsin (purple); Michigan (green).

16

Name _____

Eastern North Central States

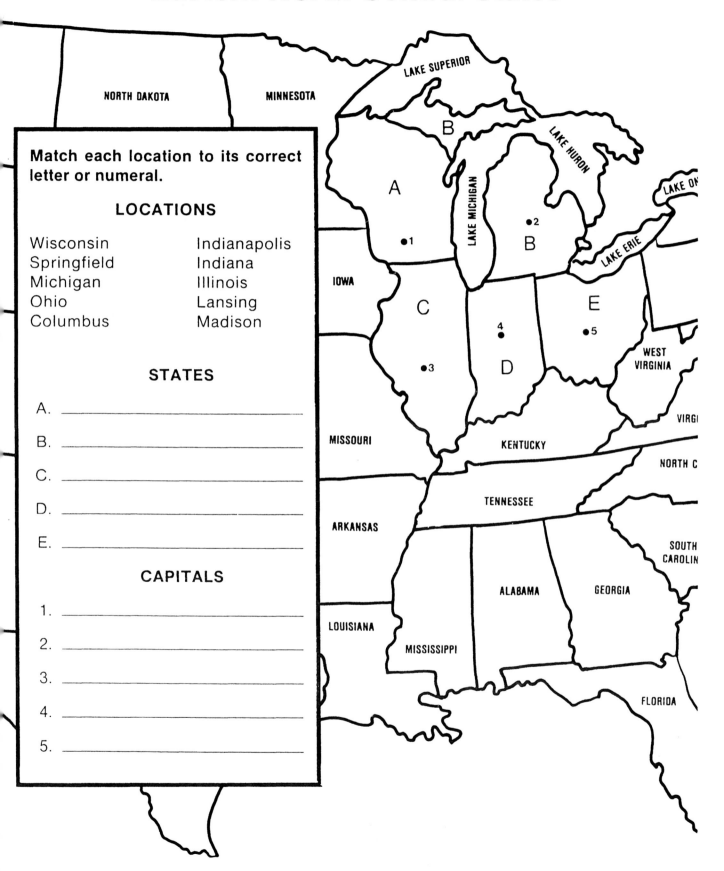

Match each location to its correct letter or numeral.

LOCATIONS

Wisconsin Indianapolis
Springfield Indiana
Michigan Illinois
Ohio   Lansing
Columbus Madison

STATES

A. _____

B. _____

C. _____

D. _____

E. _____

CAPITALS

1. _____

2. _____

3. _____

4. _____

5. _____

17

Regions of the United States

Eastern North Central States

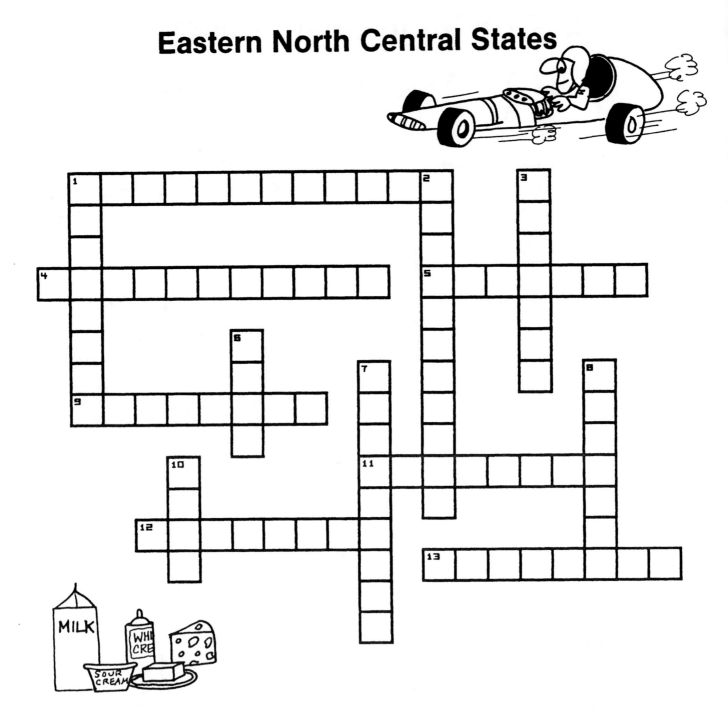

ACROSS CLUES:

1. capital of Indiana
4. river forming western boundary of Illinois
5. state between Ohio and Illinois
9. Great Lake north of Wisconsin
11. capital of Ohio
12. Lake Huron is northeast of this state.
13. Great Lake between Wisconsin and Michigan

DOWN CLUES:

1. state south of Wisconsin
2. capital of Illinois
3. capital of Wisconsin
6. Great Lake north of Ohio
7. state north of Illinois
8. capital of Michigan
10. state east of Indiana

Name _____

Eastern North Central States

Michigan is made up of two peninsulas called the Upper Peninsula and the Lower Peninsula. They are joined by the beautiful Mackinac Bridge. Most of the auto industry of the United States is located in Detroit. Michigan borders four of the Great Lakes.

Wisconsin is a state that is popular for its dairy products. This state, which has about 15,000 lakes, is a popular vacation spot. Wisconsin is also a leading producer of paper.

Indiana is the home of the famous Indianapolis Speedway. Johnny Appleseed planted many apple trees in Indiana. Gary is a famous steel city. People from Indiana are called "Hoosiers."

Ohio is a leading industrial state. Auto parts and machinery are produced there. Seven United States Presidents were born in Ohio. Astronauts John Glenn and Neil Armstrong were born in Ohio.

Illinois has the world's busiest airport, O'Hare International in Chicago. North America's tallest building, the Sears Tower, is also in Chicago. This city was almost destroyed by fire in 1871 when Mrs. O'Leary's cow kicked over a lantern. Abraham Lincoln lived in Illinois.

What did you learn?

1. Johnny Appleseed was busy planting trees in _____ .

2. _____ is the leading dairy state.

3. The tallest building in North America is the _____ _____

    located in Chicago, _____ .

4. Seven U.S. Presidents were born in _____ .

5. The U.S. auto industry is centered in _____ , Michigan.

6. The Indianapolis Speedway is located in _____ .

7. The world's busiest airport is _____

    located in _____ , Illinois.

8. Michigan's two peninsulas are joined by the _____

    _____ .

9. Abraham Lincoln lived in _____ .

10. John Glenn, a famous _____ , was from Ohio.

11. People from Indiana are called " _____ ."

12. _____ has about 15,000 lakes.

19

Eastern North Central States

Complete this puzzle with answers to the questions below.

1. I am the state located north of Illinois. What state am I?
2. I am the capital of Wisconsin. What is my name?
3. I am the state located east of Illinois. What state am I?
4. I am the capital of Illinois. What is my name?
5. I am an astronaut. My first name is Neil. What is my last name?
6. I am the bridge which joins the Upper and Lower Peninsulas of Michigan. What is my name?
7. I am a famous steel city in Indiana. What is my name?
8. The Macinack Bridge connects my two parts. What are my parts called?
9. I am the birthplace of John Glenn. What state am I?
10. I am the capital of Michigan. What is my name?
11. I am a city in Illinois that was almost destroyed by fire. What is my name?
12. I am North America's tallest building. What is my name?

What speedway is located in Indiana? (letters in the vertical box on the puzzle spell the answer.

Name _____

Southern States

1. **Write the name of each state, city, body of water, or mountain range in its correct location on the map below. Use colored pencils.**

RED	GREEN	BLACK
Alabama	Montgomery	Gulf of Mexico
Oklahoma	Baton Rouge	Appalachian Mountains
Louisiana	Little Rock	Ozark Mountains
Kentucky	Oklahoma City	Mississippi River
Mississippi	Nashville	Rio Grande River
Texas	Jackson	
Arkansas	Frankfort	
Tennessee	Austin	

2. **With colored pencils, shade in each state:** Mississippi (gray); Texas (yellow); Oklahoma (green); Arkansas (purple); Louisiana (brown); Alabama (blue); Kentucky (pink); Tennessee (orange).

21

Regions of the United States

Southern States

Match each location to its correct letter or numeral.

LOCATIONS	STATES	CAPITALS
Kentucky	A. _____	1. _____
Montgomery	B. _____	2. _____
Alabama	C. _____	3. _____
Tennessee		
Baton Rouge	D. _____	4. _____
Little Rock		
Oklahoma City	E. _____	5. _____
Mississippi		
Nashville	F. _____	6. _____
Jackson		
Frankfort	G. _____	7. _____
Austin		
Texas	H. _____	8. _____
Oklahoma		
Arkansas		
Louisiana		

22

©Remedia Publications

Southern States

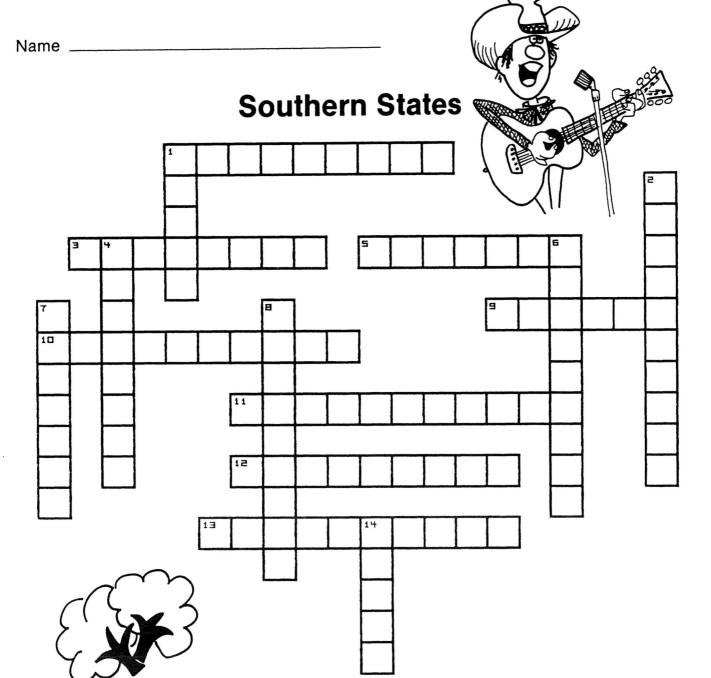

ACROSS CLUES:

1. state south of Kentucky
3. state north of Texas
5. capital of Mississippi
9. capital of Texas
10. capital of Arkansas
11. state west of Alabama
12. river between Texas and Mexico
13. capital of Alabama

DOWN CLUES:

1. state south of Oklahoma
2. capital of Louisiana
4. state north of Tennessee
6. capital of Tennessee
7. state east of Mississippi
8. state south of Arkansas
14. mountains in Arkansas

Regions of the United States

Southern States

Arkansas is famous for the springs of water which bubble throughout the state. Some contain minerals which can help cure illness and some are hot. The people living in the Ozark Mountains are known for their folk arts and crafts.

Texas is the second largest state. A famous historical battle took place at the Alamo. Davy Crockett died in this battle. Texas leads the nation in oil, sheep, and cattle production.

Oklahoma is the state shaped like a pan . The western piece of Oklahoma is called "The Panhandle." Tulsa is the oil capital of the world. The headquarters of more than 800 oil companies are located here.

Louisiana is where the famous city of New Orleans is located. Each year before Lent, a carnival called Mardi Gras is held there. Jazz also had its start in New Orleans. Cotton, rice, and sugar cane are raised in Louisiana.

Birmingham, **Alabama**, is famous for its large steel industry. It is called "The Pittsburgh of the South " Mobile is the state's only seaport. You can go surf fishing on the Gulf of Mexico when visiting Alabama.

Mississippi has many Southern plantations that tourists like to visit. There are also sandy beaches along the Gulf of Mexico. Cotton is this state's most important crop.

Tennessee is the home of Lookout Mountain. On a clear day, you can see seven states from the top of this mountain. The Grand Ole Opry is located in Nashville, the home of country music. Tourists visit the Great Smoky Mountain National Park.

Kentucky is home to more than 250 horse farms. Lexington is the horse center of America. The U.S. gold reserves are stored at Fort Knox. Mammoth Cave is also located in this state.

Where in the South would you find . . .

1. where the U.S. gold reserves are stored?

   _____

2. the Grand Ole Opry?

   _____

3. springs of healing water?

   _____

4. a place from which you could see seven states at one time?

   _____

5. where jazz began?

   _____

6. the Alamo?

   _____

7. "The Pittsburgh of the South"?

   _____

8. Southern plantations?

   _____

9. the oil capital of the world?

   _____

Southern States

```
R I O T A M D T E N N E S S E E F L E O
S O N X A S U E B A L M E G H A I V W K
X Y Z P R M E X I C O A Q Y S U B W C L
B V T D F O H A X I Z E G A L A B A M A
A R K A N S A S J X A T K X L P A M U H
T V N D A B S F Q H R I C R G L W E Y O
O C M E S O T K R B K D Z A Z J P F V M
N Q K H H G X N J U O L A S I P L N S A
R T W A V Y U Q D W Y B P Z V X O M C R
O E G M I S S I S S I P P I J F U H I L
U M T K L R K U N W P S A U S T I N O Q
G D X A L Z E E B V J F L L C R S G Y H
E S I W E K N O T P X Q A U M Z I N V Y
C G A E L I T T L E R O C K B I A F H D
P J U L B N U R D Y K T H O V C N Q S M
Y Z O R J T C X W Q A R I O G R A N D E
M B X J A C K S O N E P A A F S E G U L
K Z C H V N Y D I W M O N T G O M E R Y
```

Use these clues to find and circle the hidden words in the puzzle above.

1. a state famous for hot springs
2. the capital of Tennessee
3. state whose most important crop is cotton
4. the capital of Mississippi
5. a beautiful mountain range in Arkansas
6. the capital of Louisiana
7. state in which the Mardi Gras is held
8. the capital of Alabama
9. state located north of Tennessee

10. the capital of Arkansas
11. the large state south of Oklahoma
12. the state located north of Texas
13. state whose capital is Montgomery
14. large body of water south of Mississippi; the Gulf of _____
15. the capital of Texas
16. the river between Texas and Mexico
17. mountain range in eastern Tennessee

25

North Central States

1. **Write the name of each state, city, body of water, or mountain range in its correct location on the map below. Use colored pencils.**

RED
_____

Iowa
South Dakota
Missouri
Minnesota
Nebraska
North Dakota
Kansas

GREEN
_____

St. Paul
Topeka
Pierre
Lincoln
Jefferson City
Bismarck
Des Moines

BLACK
_____

Mississippi River
Missouri River
Black Hills
Ozark Mountains

2. **With colored pencils, shade in each state:** North Dakota (pink); South Dakota (yellow); Nebraska (green); Kansas (brown); Minnesota (blue); Iowa (orange); Missouri (purple).

North Central States

Match each location to its correct letter or numeral.

LOCATIONS

Missouri   South Dakota
Iowa   Topeka
Minnesota   Lincoln
St. Paul   Nebraska
Des Moines   Kansas
Jefferson City   Bismarck
North Dakota   Pierre

STATES

A. _____
B. _____
C. _____
D. _____
E. _____
F. _____
G. _____

CAPITALS

1. _____
2. _____
3. _____
4. _____
5. _____
6. _____
7. _____

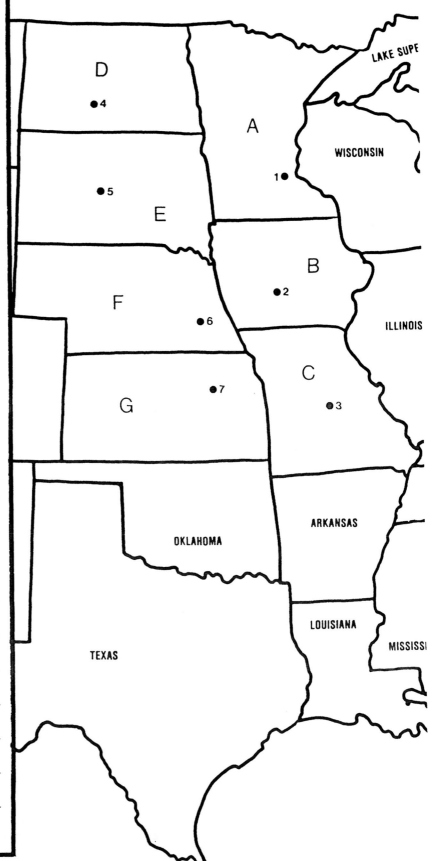

North Central States

ACROSS CLUES:

4. state northwest of Minnesota
5. state north of Arkansas
8. capital of Minnesota
11. state south of South Dakota
12. state north of Iowa
13. capital of North Dakota
14. capital of Missouri

DOWN CLUES:

1. state north of Nebraska
2. state south of Nebraska
3. capital of South Dakota
6. state south of Minnesota
7. capital of Iowa
9. capital of Kansas
10. capital of Nebraska

28

North Central States

North Dakota is the home of the Badlands, a sandstone, shale, and clay valley of beautiful and interesting shapes. Most of North Dakota is farmland and large ranches. Theodore Roosevelt owned two ranches in North Dakota.

Minnesota produces more iron than any other state. The world-famous Mayo Clinic is located in Rochester. The Mississippi River begins in Itasca State Park. Paul Bunyan and his Blue Ox are lumbering legends.

South Dakota is most famous for Mount Rushmore, located in the Black Hills. This monument has the faces of four Presidents carved in the side of a mountain. The Homestake Mine at Lead is the largest gold mine in the United States. Deadwood is an historic gold rush town.

Nebraska is where Arbor Day was started. This is a special day for planting trees. Omaha has a large meat packing industry. Boy's Town, near Omaha, is a home for neglected and homeless boys. Agriculture is the main industry in Nebraska.

Kansas is the leading wheat-producing state. It is often called "The Breadbasket of America" because it produces so much flour for the bakers of America. Abilene was the home of President Dwight Eisenhower.

Iowa is a leading producer of corn and hogs. The nation's largest popcorn plant is located in Sioux City. Education is important in Iowa, and 99 percent of the people can read and write!

Hannibal, **Missouri**, was the home of Mark Twain, the author of the book *Tom Sawyer*. The Gateway Arch in St. Louis is the world's tallest monument. It is shaped like a rainbow. The Ozark Mountains are a beautiful place for a vacation.

Name the state . . .

1. Mount Rushmore

_____

2. source of the Mississippi River

_____

3. "Breadbasket of the Nation"

_____

4. home of the Mayo Clinic

_____

5. Black Hills

_____

6. President Eisenhower's home

_____

7. The Badlands

_____

8. producer of corn and hogs

_____

9. Boy's Town

_____

10. Gateway Arch

_____

Regions of the United States

Name _____

North Central States

Complete this puzzle with answers to the questions below.

1. I am the state in which Mark Twain grew up. What state am I?
2. I am a world-famous clinic in Minnesota. What is my name?
3. I am the state located north of Nebraska. What state am I?
4. I am the leading wheat-producing state. What state am I?
5. I am the state in which the Badlands are located. What state am I?
6. I am the state north of Kansas. What state am I?
7. I am Deadwood. What kind of famous town am I?
8. I am the capital of Iowa. What is my name?
9. Kansas was my home. What U.S. President was I?
10. I am the Gateway Arch. I am the tallest of what type of building?
11. I am the city near which Boy's Town is located. What city am I?
12. I am the Great Lake which borders Minnesota. What Great Lake am I?
13. I am the state of Kansas, "The _____ of America."
    What word is missing from my nickname?

Four Presidents' heads are carved into this mountain. What is its name? (letters in the vertical box on the puzzle spell the answer)

Regions of the United States   ©Remedia Publications

Rocky Mountain States

1. **Write the name of each state, city, body of water, or mountain range in its correct location on the map below. Use colored pencils.**

RED

New Mexico
Montana
Utah
Colorado
Idaho
Arizona
Nevada
Wyoming

GREEN

Helena
Phoenix
Cheyenne
Santa Fe
Salt Lake City
Denver
Boise
Carson City

BLACK

Rocky Mountains
Great Salt Lake
Colorado River

2. **With colored pencils, shade in each state:**
    Montana (gray);
    Wyoming (blue);
    Nevada (orange);
    Colorado (green);
    Arizona (yellow);
    New Mexico (brown);
    Idaho (pink);
    Utah (purple).

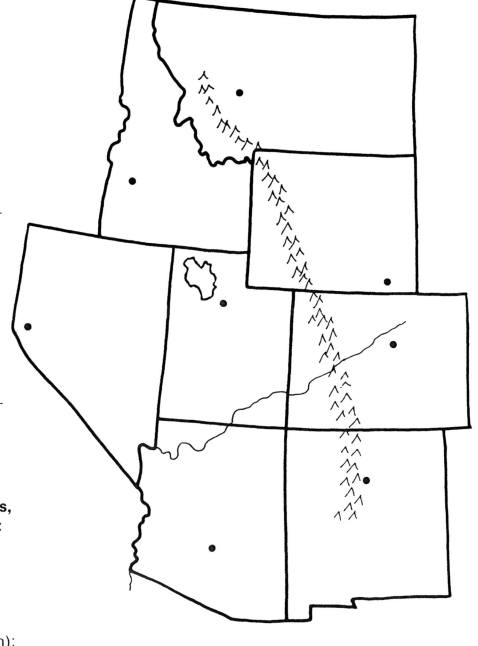

31

Regions of the United States

Name _____

Rocky Mountain States

Match each location to its correct letter or numeral.

LOCATIONS

Montana   Utah
Santa Fe   Colorado
Idaho   Carson City
Phoenix   Arizona
Wyoming   New Mexico
Denver   Cheyenne
Nevada   Boise
Salt Lake City   Helena

STATES

A. _____

B. _____

C. _____

D. _____

E. _____

F. _____

G. _____

H. _____

CAPITALS

1. _____

2. _____

3. _____

4. _____

5. _____

6. _____

7. _____

8. _____

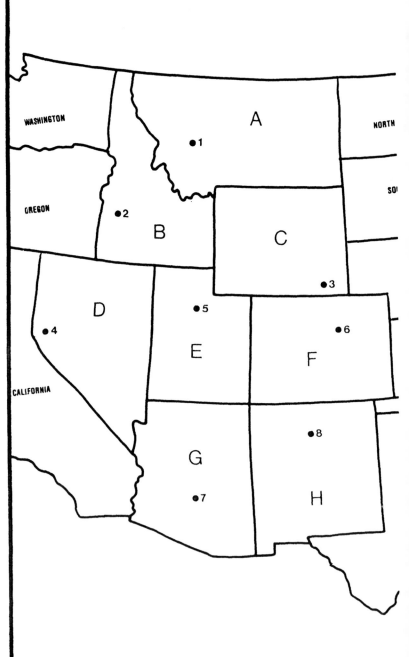

32

Name _____

Rocky Mountain States

ACROSS CLUES:

3. The _____ _____ borders Arizona.
6. The _____ Mountains stretch more than 3,000 miles.
7. most western state in this region
9. state east of Nevada
12. state south of Montana
14. capital of Arizona
15. capital of Utah
17. capital of Nevada

DOWN CLUES:

1. state north of Wyoming
2. nicknamed "The Grand Canyon State"
3. state north of New Mexico
4. state west of Montana
5. capital of Colorado
8. state east of Arizona
10. capital of Montana
11. capital of Idaho
13. capital of New Mexico
16. capital of Wyoming

33

Regions of the United States

Rocky Mountain States

New Mexico is the home of the Pueblo Indians. They are famous for their beautiful arts and crafts. Carlsbad Caverns National Park, a series of huge caves, is also in New Mexico.

Nevada, the leading producer of gold, is the driest state in the United States. Las Vegas, a famous gambling city, is in Nevada. Also in this state is Hoover Dam, one of the world's highest dams.

Idaho, the home of famous potatoes, has 22 different mountain ranges. Craters of the Moon National Monument can be found in Idaho. It has 80 square miles of formations that look like the moon.

Colorado's capital is Denver, the " Mile High City." A famous mountain in this state is Pike's Peak. Also in Colorado is the Royal Gorge, a 1,000-foot deep canyon. This canyon is crossed by the world's highest suspension bridge.

Arizona is famous for its warm, dry, sunny weather. Thousands go to this state to see the world's largest canyon, the Grand Canyon. Other scenic areas of this state are the Painted Desert and the Petrified Forest.

Wyoming has many interesting places to visit. Yellowstone Park has 200 geysers. The most famous is Old Faithful. Another place to see is beautiful Grand Teton National Park and a famous landmark called Devil's Tower.

Montana is rich in natural resources and is often called "The Treasure State." This state has many farms and ranches. Glacier Park is in Montana. It has over 50 glaciers and 250 lakes.

Utah is home to the Great Salt Lake which is so salty you won't sink if you go swimming. Most towns in this state were settled by Mormons. Also in Utah is a large copper mine in Bingham Canyon.

Where would you go to see . . .

1. Yellowstone Park?

   _____

2. The Grand Canyon?

   _____

3. The Mile High City?

   _____

4. The Great Salt Lake?

   _____

5. Glacier Park?

   _____

6. Hoover Dam?

   _____

7. Carlsbad Caverns National Park?

   _____

8. Bingham Canyon?

   _____

9. The Painted Desert?

   _____

10. Craters of the Moon Monument?

    _____

Rocky Mountain States

```
N E S A V E D E S A U M N E M C A M O S
E C G R E A T S A L T L A K E A N H D A
S T A O A M B A Y L A O X L V W F E B C
A X I C B C W K R Z H N L E A K A F V A
N E A K C S Y A S C A E O C D E N V E R
T Z O Y F L O N V H E L E N A T U T U S
N O G M T Y M T G E S E E L Y E A P H O
D P H O E N I X V Y A T I J N I R D C N
S C E U R N N C T E W E N I X M I M O C
A D M N N Q G P U N E V A D A O Z E L I
D E B T C O Q N O N G W H A A I O T O T
A I S A N T A F E E M R K H R J N O R Y
N R S I O R R T E Y O S M O N T A N A W
T S N N E W M E X I C O F Z X H Y C D G
B O I S E E I A G O L C O K A H L I O N
```

Use these clues to find and circle the hidden words in the puzzle above.

1. the "Treasure State"
2. home of the Hoover Dam
3. state famous for potatoes
4. state in which the Carlsbad Caverns are located
5. a beautiful mountain range
6. a large lake found in Utah
7. the capital of Arizona
8. state that was settled by Mormons
9. the capital of Montana

10. the capital of Nevada
11. the Mile High City
12. the capital of New Mexico
13. the capital of Wyoming
14. state in which the Grand Canyon is located
15. state in which the Grand Teton National Park is located
16. the capital of Idaho
17. home of Pike's Peak

35

Regions of the United States

Pacific States

1. **Write the name of each state, city, body of water, or mountain range in its correct location on the map below. Use colored pencils.**

RED

Washington
California
Hawaiian Islands
Oregon
Alaska

GREEN

Juneau
Salem
Olympia
Sacramento
Honolulu

BLACK

Mt. McKinley
Columbia River
Pacific Ocean
Yukon River

2. **With colored pencils, shade in each state:**
Alaska (blue);
Hawaiian Islands (green);
California (yellow);
Oregon (orange);
Washington (pink).

Name _____

Pacific States

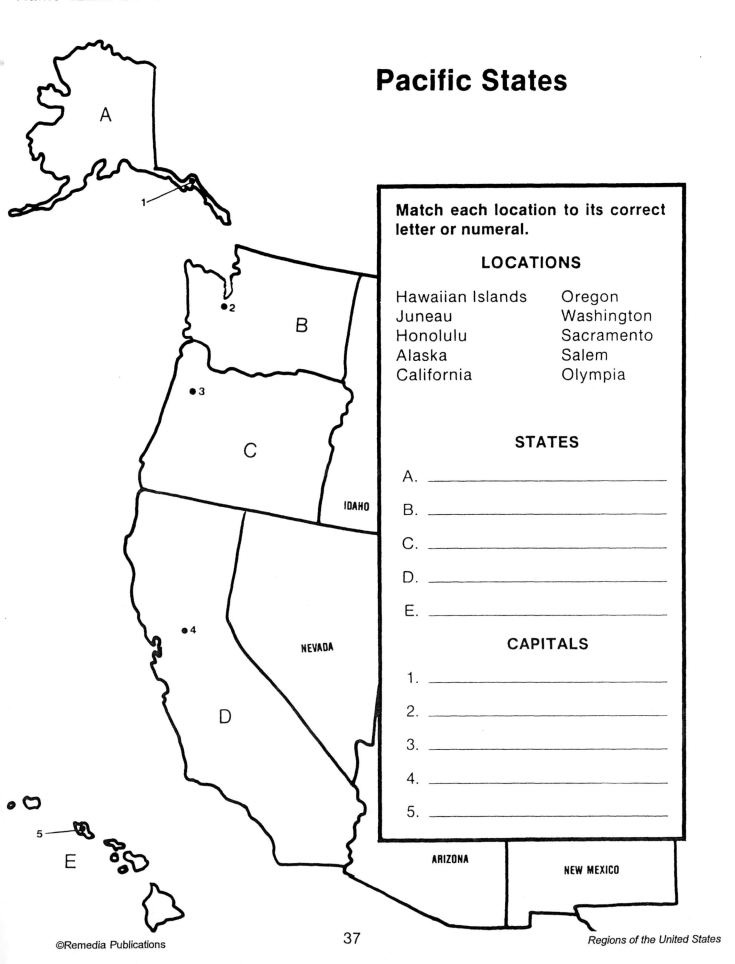

Match each location to its correct letter or numeral.

LOCATIONS

Hawaiian Islands	Oregon
Juneau	Washington
Honolulu	Sacramento
Alaska	Salem
California	Olympia

STATES

A. _____

B. _____

C. _____

D. _____

E. _____

CAPITALS

1. _____

2. _____

3. _____

4. _____

5. _____

IDAHO

NEVADA

ARIZONA

NEW MEXICO

Regions of the United States

Pacific States

ACROSS CLUES:

1. state south of Oregon
4. capital of Hawaii
8. capital of California
9. largest state
10. capital of Alaska
11. river in Alaska
12. state south of Washington

DOWN CLUES:

1. river between Washington and Oregon
2. capital of Washington
3. state north of Oregon
4. over 100 islands
5. capital of Oregon
6. mountain in Alaska
7. ocean west of Oregon

Pacific States

California has more people than any other state. If you visit this state, you can see Yosemite Park, Hollywood, Disneyland, and the world's tallest trees.

Oregon leads all other states in the production of lumber. Portland is the state's largest city. Crater Lake, the deepest lake in the United States, is in Oregon.

Hawaii is made up of over 100 islands that stretch for 1,600 miles. These islands are the tops of volcanoes that rise from the bottom of the Pacific Ocean. Pearl Harbor, in Hawaii, was attacked by Japan on December 7, 1941.

Alaska is the largest of the 50 states. It was bought from Russia in 1867 for $7,000,000, or about two cents an acre. Mt. McKinley is the highest mountain in the United States. Alaska has the smallest population of all the states.

Washington is the only state named for a U.S. President. Seattle is the largest city. Many shipyards are located around Puget Sound. Washington leads the states in apple production.

What did you learn?

1. _____ has more people than any other state.

2. Crater Lake, the deepest lake in the United States, is located in

   _____ .

3. The largest of the 50 states is _____ .

4. A state made up of over 100 islands is _____ .

5. A state famous for its production of apples is _____ .

6. The world's tallest trees can be seen in _____ .

7. Pearl Harbor is in _____ .

8. _____ has fewer people than any other state.

9. Puget Sound is in _____ .

10. _____ leads all other states in the production of lumber.

11. The Hawaiian Islands are the tops of _____ .

12. In 1867, the United States bought Alaska from _____ .

Regions of the United States

Pacific States

Complete this puzzle with answers to the questions below.

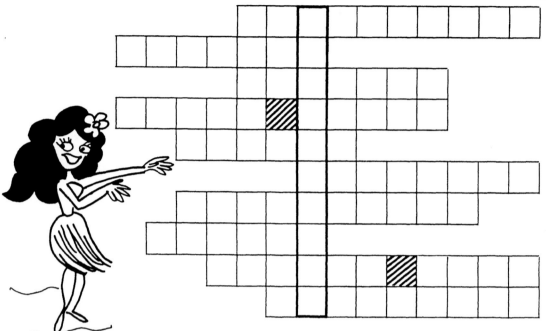

1. I am the only state named after a U.S. President. What state am I?

2. I am the capital of Washington. What city am I?

3. I am the ocean west of California. What ocean am I?

4. I am a river in Alaska. What is my name?

5. I am the capital of Alaska. What city am I?

6. I am a famous mountain in Alaska. What mountain am I?

7. I am a famous amusement park in California. What is my name?

8. I am the state south of Washington. What state am I?

9. I am the deepest lake in the United States. What lake am I?

10. We formed the islands of Hawaii. What are we?

I am the capital of California. What city am I? (letters in the vertical box on the puzzle spell the answer)

Regions of the United States   ©Remedia Publications

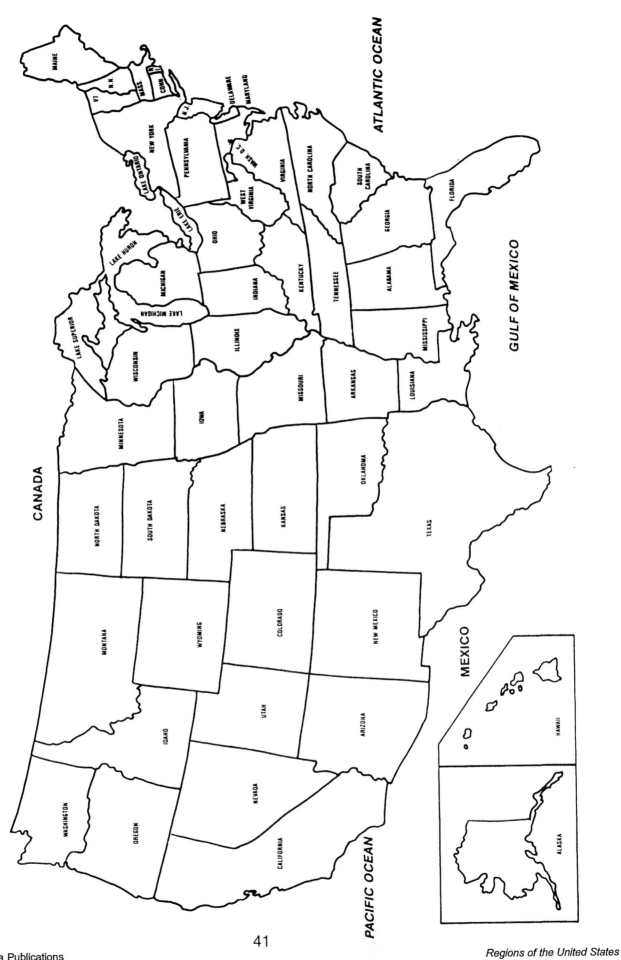

Regions of the United States

Regions of the U.S. - State Data Sheet

Use an encyclopedia to find the following information about your state.

1. Name of state: _____

2. Region in which it is located (New England, Mid-Atlantic, South Atlantic, Eastern North Central, Southern, North Central, Rocky Mountain, Pacific):

    _____

3. Capital city: _____

4. Year of statehood: _____

5. Population of state (round off to nearest 1,000): _____

6. Largest city in state: _____

7. Size (area in square miles): _____

8. State nickname: _____

9. State bird: _____

10. State flower: _____

11. State tree: _____

12. Two-letter postal abbreviation: _____

13. Major farm product or natural resource: _____

14. Major industry: _____

15. Terrain (List as many as apply: desert, plateau, mountains, plains, etc.)

    _____

16. List two interesting places to visit in this state.

    _____

    _____

42